Marcenus Wright

The moral aphorisms and terseological teachings of Confucius

A correct likeness of the great philosopher, and a short sketch of his life

Marcenus Wright

The moral aphorisms and terseological teachings of Confucius
A correct likeness of the great philosopher, and a short sketch of his life

ISBN/EAN: 9783743376915

Manufactured in Europe, USA, Canada, Australia, Japa

Cover: Foto ©Thomas Meinert / pixelio.de

Manufactured and distributed by brebook publishing software
(www.brebook.com)

Marcenus Wright

The moral aphorisms and terseological teachings of Confucius

THE

MORAL APHORISMS

AND

TERSEOLOGICAL TEACHINGS

OF

'CONFUCIUS,

THE SAPIENT CHINESE PHILOSOPHER,

WHO LIVED FIVE HUNDRED AND FIFTY-ONE YEARS BEFORE
THE CHRISTIAN ERA, AND WHOSE WISE PRECEPTS
HAVE LEFT A LASTING IMPRESSION UPON ALL
SUBSEQUENT CIVILIZED NATIONS.

TO WHICH IS ADDED

A CORRECT LIKENESS OF THE GREAT PHILOSOPHER,

AND

A SHORT SKETCH OF HIS LIFE.

By M. R. K. Wright.

BATTLE CREEK, MICH.:
PUBLISHED FOR THE AUTHOR.
1870.

REVIEWER'S PREFACE.

In presenting a newly-revised edition of the time-honored Precepts of Confucius to the public, we hope to meet with the approval of the admirers of that wise and truth-loving ancient philosopher and political economist. Our author lived the life of a just and noble man, and left a heritage of personal greatness behind him, in his moral essays, which Chinese admiration still upholds as the only worthy standard of justice, by which all men should be governed in the pursuit of those mutual relations and duties which pertain to human existence and happiness.

The aphorisms of Confucius are worthy of the highest recognition and commendation from all well-inclined and thoughtful men, and are only equaled by the precepts of the great Christian Master who rested the superstructure of his moral philosophy upon the identical "Golden Rule" which is the basic principle of Confucianism.

The object of re-arranging and newly wording

the sentiments embodied in the maxims of our author at the present time, is to be found in the increased demand for a high moral literature, of which Confucius is acknowledged to be a disciple in the wisest light of mind.

The author has accumulated facts and data during many years past, with the ultimate design of enlarging and improving the little volume of wise sayings which have been translated from the Chinese of KONG-FU-TSE, and which found a cast-about existence in England many years ago, and subsequently in very imperfect form by the present authority in America.

The life of the sage of Lu, as herein presented, is newly written and modified to conform to more recent historic disclosures, and facts derived from encyclopedian sources; while the portrait of Confucius is taken from the illustrated work of Pauthier, which is the only veritable key to the manners, customs, literature, and opinions, of the ancient Chinese.

When a great and good man makes his *debut* upon the stage of human experience, and lives a life of unimpugned justice and honor, it becomes our duty, as admirers or advocates of the principles which he taught, to frankly acknowledge our indebtedness therefor, as well as to understand the personal peculiarities which distinguished our esteemed exemplar above the ordinary condition of men.

The social and political systems of China are founded upon the methodical aphorisms of the *Le-king* and *Ta-heo*, the two principal books of the Confucian Philosophy, which is professed by all her greatest men, and accepted as the principal belief of all the educated classes.

Confucius was a pungent maximist of unexceptionable character, and has been the worthy recipient of the laudations of his numerous countrymen during the period of twenty-five centuries which have intervened since his decease. The fullness of his love of justice, as manifested in his exemplary life and teachings, *has no equal* in the annals of moralistic history. His wondrous adoration of the principle of goodness may be regarded as almost a miraculous expression of human wisdom, and his worship of the Omnipotent Architect of nature, as the highest and noblest form of rationalistic veneration.

When we contemplate the vast amount of time which separates us from the originator of the most astute civil and religious philosophy ever given to mankind, and remember the disadvantages which then interposed to cancel his claim to superior discernment and sagacity as a teacher and counsellor of his nation, we may not only hold the "light of hope" in our own hands, as the cherished sentiment of the future, but regarding the sage precepts of Confucius as both timely and acceptable to the literature of the age, we may experience an ever-increasing thankfulness for his success as the REDEEMER of the Mongolian race.

LIFE OF CONFUCIUS.

THE celebrated Chinese sage who bore the name of Kong, meaning master or teacher, or KONG-FU-TSE, as given by his disciples, and afterward Latinized into Confucius by certain Jesuit missionaries who resided in China during the latter part of the seventeenth century, was born at Shangping, near the town of Tseuse, in the petty kingdom of Lu, on the 19th day of June, B. C. 551.

His mother, whose name was Yan-she, and who is said to have sprung from the illustrious family of Yen, used to call her son by the singular name of Kieu—which signifies, in the Mongolian language, a "little hillock" or protuberance—because he had an unusual elevation on the top of his forehead, in the region of comparison, benevolence, and love of nature, as defined by modern phrenologists. Various prophecies and forerunners of his birth and destiny, as we are told, are to be found in the annals of Chinese literature, and his worldly coming and career are said to have been revealed by the seers of earlier ages; but this is a question as improbable, in the light of reflection, as the uncertainty of many similar prophetic disclosures concerning men and things in other times, and among other nations, and may be received with a wise allowance in favor of absolute knowledge.

A renowned pedigree has been attributed to Confucius by his disciples, who derive his origin

from Ho-ang-ti, a distinguished monarch who is
said to have reigned in China 2000 years before
the Christian era, or cotemporaneously with the
fourth and sixth Egyptian Dynasties under the
rule of the younger Pharaohs. His father, whose
name was Shuh-le-ang-ho, died when Confucius
was only three years old. But Yan-she, his lov-
ing mother, extended to him her watchful care,
and he received from her hand that attention and
training which, associated with his naturally well-
inclined disposititon, soon gave assurance of a
manhood wherein indications of unusual mental
qualities were presented. From his earliest years,
he manifested an extraordinary love for intellect-
ual pursuits, and displayed a deep and abiding
interest in, and veneration for, the time-honored
laws of his native country.

Philosophic gravity, moral rectitude, and considerate deportment, marked his conduct when a
boy, and won for him that extollation which was
so characteristic of his entire life. He was grave
and serious, yet pleasant, in his appearance, and
took but little delight in playing and running
about for amusement and pastime as was the habit
of most boys of his own age.

It is also said of Confucius that his knowledge
was intuitive; and that he seemed to arrive at
just and legitimate conclusions with wondrous
ease, while yet the faculties of his mind were
hardly released from the insecurity of infancy.
But his unexampled and exalted goodness was the
distinguishing trait of his character, and his fidelity to a just decision of mind was always uppermost and unflinching. He esteemed, and confided
in, his relatives, and made it his duty to receive
the counsel and follow the advice of his grand-

father, who was then living in the kingdom of
Lu, at a very advanced age, and who was regarded by all who knew him as a man in the exercise of worthy sobriety, probity, and honor.

It is related by one of the biographers of Confucius, that when he was a boy in his fifth year
of age, being in the presence of his grandfather
whom he heard sighing, he approached him with
happy consideration and a full heart, and said,
"May I presume, without being deprived of your
respect, to inquire into the occasion of your sorrow? Perhaps you regard your posterity as likely
to degenerate, and wander from the exercise of
that virtue and desirable righteousness which you
so much admire." Whereupon Coum-tse, for such
was his grandfather's name, being somewhat surprised at the sympathy and precocity of thought
manifested by the young philosopher, very quietly
replied, "What suggested that thought in your
mind, my dear boy? and where have you learned
to think and speak so wisely?" "From yourself,"
answered Confucius. "I usually regard your conversation, and I have many times heard you remark that it is a duty a son owes to his ancestors,
to support their virtuous habits and good name,
or he proves himself unworthy of a record in the
annals of their fame."

After the death of his grandfather, Confucius
became the pupil of Tcem-se, a renowned thinker
and scholar of his time. Under the guidance of
so wise a tutor, he soon made a surprising advancement in the matter of his studies. The subject of primitive history, or the antiquity of his
race, was made the theme of interesting consideration and remark, and he considered it as the

source from which was to be derived much valuable information.

His stubborn regard for the ancients often caused him serious disputes and difficulties; and it is related that upon one occasion, when only in his sixteenth year of age, he came very near losing his life in consequence of engaging in a discussion—concerning certain Chinese books which treated of the subject of antiquity—with a bigoted person of high rank and quality, who insisted that they were obscure, and unworthy of the time employed in their consideration. " The books which you despise," said Confucius, " are full of profound knowledge, which is not to be obtained without desire and the relinquishment of unwise prejudice. The subordination of spirits by which the ignorant are made dependent upon the cohorts of the Imperial Register, may seem best to the sordid and indifferent, but to the liberal and the just, however poor, the righteousness of ancient simplicity and sobriety is no longer a question of doubt. Only a short time since, an ordinary person with whom I was in conversation expressed similar sentiments to those which you have uttered. At that I was not surprised; but I am astonished that one of your rank and learning should qualify your opinions as one of the lowest of the people."

Confucius was subject to reprehension for his conversation with a peer of the realm, in the light of individual impertinence, and was threatened with severe penalties if he persisted in a continuance of such discussions.

At the age of nineteen he received the appointment of inspector of the corn-marts, and became very much distinguished by the manifestation of great industry and energy in suppressing fraud and dishonesty in trade, and by the timely introduction of desirable order and integrity into all the business relations over which he held control.

At the age of nineteen years, he was married; but at the end of four years released himself from matrimonial life, as it is said, that he might be free from all household incumbrances and connections, and at liberty to propagate his already widely-known philosophy throughout the empire. He is reported, by his biographers, to have lived contentedly with his wife while it was her happiness to be his consort, and refused himself the privilege of keeping concubines, which was then the common custom of his country, because he believed it objectionable in the light of a wise understanding of Nature's intention.

Confucius received the appointment of inspector-general of pastures and flocks; and the result of the judicious measures which he instituted to regulate the production of live stock, which was then an important and profitable occupation for the husbandman, and a direct source of revenue to the government, was clearly manifest in the improvement and progress made in the cultivation of the country, and in the condition of the people.

The mother of our moral hero died when he was in his twenty-third year; and, owing to his affectionate regard for her, and the ancestral family from which she derived her name, he allowed his excessive grief to interfere for a time with the discharge of his administrative duties; and finally, in obedience to a well-considered determination of mind, he resigned the functions of his office altogether, and gave himself up to solemn retirement, which was the first important act marking

his career as a pure-minded and honest philosopher.

In conformity to a custom which had long been
held in derision by many of his countrymen, and
which had been derived from very remote periods,
he made the ceremony of the burial of his mother
the occasion of great splendor, as well as solemnity, a deviation from the prevailing quiet method,
which struck his courtiers and fellow-citizens with
equal wonder and astonishment, but which they
appeared better satisfied to accept than to reject.
And, as a consequence of their satisfaction, it
soon became the habit of the people to honor the
interment of the dead with ostentatious display,
in accordance with ancient rites and ceremonies.
Thus the example which he offered in his native
province, being made the subject of general sur-
prise and remark, was soon accepted by all the
neighboring States, and eventually became the
custom of the whole nation, with the exception of
the more indigent classes, and has continued to
be the practice up to the present time.

Confucius, having gained considerable knowledge in regard to antiquities, and, having formed
an extensive acquaintance with men, began to be
accepted as a wise authority in regard to the past,
and as such, ventured to communicate his opinions to the people. He advocated the necessity
of ceremonial homage, and a manifestation of
kindly respect for the departed, either in the
dwelling-house of the mourners, or at the place of
burial. From his recognition and recommendation of this ancestral usage, sprang the anni-
versary feasts which have ever since distinguished
the Chinese as a nation.

During the three years subsequent to the death

of his mother, he passed his time in close con-
finement and solitude, and engaged in the pursuit
of philosophic studies. While thus retired from
the trials, troubles, and business cares, which had
devolved upon him in his performance of public
obligations, he is said to have thoroughly reflected
upon the subject of moral precepts and principles, tracing them to their source as divinely instituted, regarding them as exampled in nature,
and inseparably associated therewith as the holy
expression of the Omnific Being, whose wise purposes could only be known as deeply inlaid in the
incessant activities and material evidences of outward existence.

Feeling imbued with these opinions, and entertaining a comprehensive sense of the duties and
requirements which they indiscriminately impose
upon all men ; and, being impressed with a con-
viction of the necessity of aiding his countrymen
to a more perfect knowledge of the " better way
of life," he concluded to make them the unvary-
ing rule and essential motive of all his actions ;
and, as a consequence of such determination, his
career was ever after marked by practical illus-
trations of the ethical system of philosophy which
he taught.

At the present time all the kingdoms of the
Chinese empire repose upon the rule of the emperor. But, during the time of Confucius, every
province was an independent State, being governed by laws of its own choice, and by a prince
of its own selection. Hence it not unfrequently
happened that the imperial authority proved in-
sufficient to keep them within the sphere of their
allegiance, and to the performance of those mutual duties and obligations which the Republican

State owes to the head of the nation. And more especially was this the case at the time of which we speak, owing to the existence of that luxuriousness of habit, love of pleasure, and general dissoluteness of manners, which prevailed in the several courts of the interior provinces.

Confucius, being wisely persuaded that the people could never be happy so long as avarice, ambition, voluptuousness, and false policy, reigned among them, resolved to advocate a rigid system of morality ; and, consequently, he commenced to instruct them in the noble precepts of philosophy which he so deeply cherished. He inspired his followers with a love for temperance, sobriety, justice, and other virtues, a contempt for riches and outward pomp, and induced them to fashion their lives to accord with a more acceptable magnanimity of mind. He everywhere objected to the practice of dissimulation and insincerity, and used all the means at his command to redeem his people from a life of pleasure and extremeisms. He was everywhere well received, and as universally beloved. His extensive knowledge and great wisdom enabled him to cope with his adversaries, and his integrity, and the splendor of his virtues, secured him that acceptance and respect which he had little anticipated. Kings were governed by his counsel, and the people reverenced him as a saint. He was favored with several high offices in the magistracy of government, but never accepted them from a motive of personal ambition or preferment, but always with a view of reforming a corrupt State, and amending the laws of his country, for the purpose of improving the condition of its people ; a fact made doubly certain by his resignation of those offices as soon as he perceived that his service therein was no longer useful to them. He corrected many frauds and abuses in the mercantile trade, and reduced the weights and measures provided for the sale of the various products of the soil to a fixed and uniform standard. He inculcated fidelity and candor among men, as needful to all happy social relations, and exhorted the women to chastity and simplicity of manners. By methods thus employed, he succeeded in producing a general reformation, and establishing such concord and unanimity of feeling and opinion, that the people of the whole kingdom seemed imbued with a higher respect for just and noble principles.

Some of the neighboring princes began to manfest symptoms of decided jealousy, believing that the emperor, under the counsels of such a man as Confucius, would soon render himself too powerful, as against the local interests of the magistrates of the nation, and as a supporter of those radical improvements and changes in the laws of the land, which they regarded as obnoxious and insecure, and which they feared might be recommended and too hastily urged upon the people of the several States. Alarmed at this condition of affairs, and knowing that the sympathies of the king were confided to the decisions of Confucius, the governor of Tsi, being a man of artful political inclinations, and much opposed to progressive reforms, resolved to assemble his ministers, and take into consideration the question of the important changes which were being effected throughout the country, and to thereby determine whether some measures might not be adopted to stay their progress.

The assembly was called, and after long and serious deliberation, resolved upon the following contemptible and debasing expedient, as the only means left them by which to thwart the continually-increasing influence and power of the advancing politico-moral philosophy: They employed the services of a large number of young and beautiful syrens, who had received instruction from their infancy in the arts of singing and dancing, and who were complete mistresses of all the charms and accomplishments which might attract attention and captivate the heart. Under the pretext of an embassy, these coquettish Chinese Bayaderes were presented to the king of Lu, and to the grandees of his court, and were received with marked favor and respect. The artful machinations conceived and projected in the council convened by Tsi, were thus early brought to public notice, and in a great measure succeeded in staying the advancement of those redemptory principles which were everywhere being accepted with such favor by the people. The duties pertaining to the administration of government were soon neglected, and little was thought of, with the exception of inventing additional pleasures, and means of entertaining fair strangers. In short, nothing was regarded, for some months, but feasting, dancing, and shows; and the court of the kingdom of Lu became wholly involved in luxury and pleasure.

Confucius had foreseen all this, and endeavored to thwart the accomplishment of so injurious an example, by advising the king to object to the inauguration of so low and debasing a series of festivities; and he earnestly labored to expose the delusion which had been imposed upon him and his courtiers, and endeavored, by every honest means to bring them back to the exercise of reason and their duty. But passion reigned triumphant; and all his efforts to redeem them from the mischief into which they had but too willingly fallen, proved wholly useless and ineffectual. The honor and severity of the philosopher were obliged to yield to the overbearing fashion of the court, controlled as it was by the unjust plans and connivance of the bitterest enemies of reform. Considering his own safety and happiness, therefore, he immediately released himself from his employment, and, leaving his native State, sought to find in other kingdoms, minds and dispositions better prepared to accept and advocate his moral doctrines.

He journeyed through the provinces of Lun, Guci, and Tson ; but meeting with unexpected difficulties, and finding many obstacles in the way of his success, he realized the inability of man to hastily fashion the inclinations of a people to suit the better purposes of human life. As a natural consequence of the indifference manifested by many of the nobility, and the temporarily-increasing tendency in certain quarters to suppress the advancement of free thought and liberal principles, as well as the growing disposition to engage in destructive pleasures and amusements, disruptions, rebellions, wars, and tumults, soon raged throughout the empire.

Thus Confucius was made aware that, for a time, the propagation of his cherished philosophy would be attended with many trials and difficulties. Men gave themselves no time to listen to the teachings of their moral master or his followers. Indeed, they had no preference for so doing, being rather inclined to worldly ambition, avarice, and corrupt manners. Hence he often met with ill-treatment, abuse, and reproachful language, at the hands of the populace, who were urged on in their malicious conduct, and evil purposes, by the ruling magistrates and the more immediate officers of their appointment.

To such an extent, at one time, were these intrigues carried, that it is historically certain that very serious conspiracies were formed against his life; to which may be added the fact that his determinate purpose to advocate the moral sentiments which he deemed essential to the welfare of the people, and advance his principles of philosophy throughout the empire of his native continent, had necessitated unlooked-for expenditures; and in the absence of a proper attention to his individual interests, he had become reduced to the extremest poverty. Some philosophers among his cotemporaries were so affected by this terrible state of affairs, that they rusticated themselves into the mountains and deserts as the only places where they could secure peace and happiness. Confucius was many times requested to follow their example, and retire from the confusion and insecurity which surrounded him. But, "I am a man, said he, "and cannot exclude myself from the society of men, to consort with wild beasts. Bad as the times are, I shall do all I can to recall men to virtue; for in virtue we may find safety and repose; and if mankind would earnestly embrace it, and submit themselves to its disciplining influence, they would need no instruction from me or any one else, to aid them in securing that hoped-for wisdom and felicity which cancels every mischief and misery in life." "It is the duty of

every man," continued he, "first to perfect himself, and then to aid in perfecting others. Human
nature came to us as an unavoidable inheritance;
and it is only in the subjugation of our evil passions and demoralizing propensities, that we are
enabled to find that happy and harmonious condition of life which we all so much desire to enjoy,
and which is the only real security against social
wrongs, personal injustice, or national distrust.
Love your neighbor as yourself. Let reason be
the guide and rule of your conduct. Speak pru-
dently, and behave worthily, upon all occasions,
and let your example be so set before all men,
that their approval of it may hold them to a love
of its practical continuance ; and the cause of our
despair and disagreement will be obliterated, while
well-to-do inclinations and individual progress will
mark our peace and prosperity, and guarantee us
that satisfaction in the success of our teachings,
which, in the present disordered social state, it is
as impossible to secure as it is unwise to expect."

Thus, although he had withdrawn himself from
kings and palaces, he did not cease to travel about
the country as a teacher and adviser of the people. His disciples were chiefly confined to the
nobility, and the social circles of the educated
and aristocratic, although he had numerous adher-
ents among the lower classes.

He is said to have had seven thousand disciples
who were earnest advocates and exemplars of his
moral doctrines; and seventy-two of this number
were distinguished above the rest by their superior
attainments, while twelve were particularly noted
for their comprehensive views and more perfect
knowledge of all the details of his philosophy.
He divided his disciples into four classes, who in-

terested themselves—respectively in accordance
with their capacity—in the propagation of the
moral doctrines which he everywhere enunciated.
The first class were advised to improve their minds
by meditation, and purify their hearts by virtue,
and thereby fashion a righteous example for the
benefit of others. The second class were to cul-
tivate the faculty of reason, making their lives
conform to the decisions of logical inference, as
presented in the practical requirements of life,
and the arguments of elegant and persuasive dis-
course. The study of the third class was to be
confined to an understanding and explanation of
the rules of good government, that the Mandarins
might be instructed in the duties pertaining to
public affairs, and fill their offices with trust and
honor. The fourth class were concerned in the
advocacy of the principles of morality, and their
delivery to the common people in a concise and
acceptable form. These were the zealous disciples, of the least number, who were regarded as
the wise apostles of the Confucian school, and
who linked their career in closest unity of purpose
with that of its distinguished founder.

Six hundred of his disciples were dispatched
into various portions of the empire at different
times, to reform the prevailing objectionable manners of the populace. And, not satisfied with
benefiting his own country, he contemplated the
propagation of his opinions in foreign lands; but,
owing to the difficulty of interpreting his thoughts
into the language of other nations, his advancing
years, and other timely reasons, these projected
schemes seem to have ultimated in no practical
benefit to himself or others, and were soon forgot-
ten in view of the many duties which accumulated

upon his hands, as the father of the most worthy and noted philosophy developed during the earlier periods of Chinese history, or ever known to mankind.

The life of Confucius is marked by the purest practical habits, and nothing may be added to the just, moral principles which he represented in his daily dealings with men. In his advocacy of "wise precepts," he seemed to speak rather as an exponent of a studied system of morality than as an inspired teacher or revelator; and, although his ideas of practical justice and morality were as pure and perfect as any that were ever uttered by the sages of the past, it is not our province to determine how far or how much of his teachings are to be regarded as intuitive, or attributable to "influx of thought" from interior or psychologic sources. In his rigorous abstemiousness, in his great sobriety and solemnity of manners, in his contempt of riches, and what are commonly denominated the "goods of life," and in his continual attention and watchfulness over his own actions and conduct, and, above all, in his exceeding humility, modesty, and courtesy, Confucius stands conspicuous as the unyielding moral philosopher who has no equal in the annals of national history, and who is worthily entitled to the credit of being regarded as the most acceptable axiomatic teacher of wise opinions whom the world has ever known.

In his life he was ever a sorrowing child of nature, and was frequently known to weep over the mistakes and follies of mankind. During the latter part of his earthly career, he became most deeply saddened and dejected, owing to the impossibility of succeeding to the extent of his desire in arousing his countrymen from the immoral languor into which they had fallen as a result of unwise counsel, evil rulers, and the discords which then prevailed throughout the empire.

A few days before his final illness, he remarked to his disciples, with tears in his eyes, that he was considerably unhappy in consequence of the disorders which existed in his native land. "The evidences," said he, "of my effort to remove the mischievous hindrances to human advancement and progress are little regarded, and the moral principles which we have labored so earnestly to make the ægis of social defense, and the standard of good government, are, for the time being, in a great measure placed under the ban of artful surveillance. The kings reject my maxims; and since I am no longer useful to my kinsmen, I pray to be released from further cares and trials. And as I feel my indebtedness to nature, I experience no greater happiness than when contemplating the prospect of my speedy release from the present solicitous condition of existence."

Confucius grew weaker day by day, until at length he completely failed of his bodily strength, and, becoming lethargic, slept himself into unconsciousness of outward life, dying in the year 478 B. C., in the seventy-third year of his age.

When Nagi-cong, who was then the ruling sovereign in the kingdom of Lu, first heard of his death, it is said that he could not restrain his inclination to weep. "The Tien is not satisfied with me," said he, "since it has taken away my Confucius." Immediately after his demise, and surprising as it may appear in view of the demoralization of his cotemporaries, Confucius began to be lamented, and his name, which was on every tongue, was adorned with golden commendation. Temples were soon built in the several provinces to accommodate the learned who gathered therein at stated seasons to pay him that homage which was justly due to his great wisdom and exceeding goodness. Upon many edifices raised to his honor in the empire are characteristic inscriptions in the symbols of the Chinese language, which are dedicatory, and signify, "To the Wisé Teacher," "To the Noble Sage," "To the Blessed Saint," "To the Tutor of Emperor and Kings," and "To the Honored Renderer of Moral Precepts." His sepulcher was raised near the city of Keo-fou, on the banks of the river Su, where his inclinations led him to assemble his disciples many times during the period of his life, for the purpose of deliberation, consultation, and the furtherance of that good work which had engaged his undivided attention for so many years.

Confucius was a reformer of the most positive school; and his system of philosophy is the most deeply imbedded in, as well as the most faithful expression of, the Chinese mind. His great ambition was confined to the re-establishment of the religion of his ancestors, which he regarded as pure and exemplary; and in this opinion he was well sustained by the evidences which had been transmitted through many generations, from the time of the monarchial reign of Hoang-ti, upward of two thousand years before the Christian era.

His teachings are justly entitled to the merit of being considered as compounded of worthy religious sentiments and well-organized philosophical considerations, including a vein of spiritual thought as based upon logical deductions and inference, presented in the Jan-za of nature. His system was more confined to social and political interests and requirements, and to the immediate wants and needs of his people and his country, than to the inculcation of the theological tenets. In fact, his belief concerning the future life and the demands of the spiritual part of man, were questions more regarded as a matter for private reflection and the decisions of individual judgment, than as subjects of special and of malignant debate. He attached no personality to Deity as disconnected with the manifestations of nature, and in his effort to fathom the mysteries associated with the existence of God, he resolved to consider the subject of his being as inscrutable as it was infallible. The all-pervading element of divine life, which was the cause of the ever-present law, order, and intelligence, displayed in the creations of the outward world, was denominated Shang-te, which literally signifies the essence, or, in other words, the Spirit of Omnipotence, as conditioned in, and exhibited through, the instrumentality of the material elements and compounds of the visible universe; and the Tien, or firmament, was supposed to be the external emblem or counterpart of his being.

Confucius employed language which would seem to imply that Shang-te possessed a majestic intelligence, and exercised a noble authority in his government; and he is represented as imposing a corrective influence, which some have interpreted to signify direct punishment for evil-doing, but which, taking the common explanation of the best educated Chinese scholars, is rendered in a very different sense, and would involve redemption through the trials, tribulations, and lessons of life.

His thoughts were confined to an indefinite conception of man's immortality; and while he believed in the existence of angels or intercessory spirits, his knowledge of the real relation of the interior to the external world, seems to have been limited or obscured by his greater attention to that philosophy or system of moral teachings, which he regarded as more directly essential or applicable to the demands of human life. He recognized the future, not as demanding our fear or humiliation, but rather our love and reverence; and our transmundane interests he held as strictly conditioned in immortal success, or that life which was hoped for, or presumed to be held in abeyance of divine purpose.

Confucius may only be considered as a wise moralist, who was ever inclined to be just; and to represent that fullness of manly habit which is seldom a characteristic of men. Unlike Christ or the apostles, he entrenched himself in the deep channels of Nature's *outward* demands, in the advocacy of needed reforms, rather than appeal to the spiritual or future interests of the soul, as a source of human improvement. The abstract idea, which formerly found a prominent place in human belief, of a creation organized out of *nothing*, by an infinite and eternal Being, with the object, that his greatness and glory might be seen and known, in the magnificence of all eternal symbols, by those intelligent creatures whom in his condescension he had deigned to create, is unknown to the Confucian system of ethical doctrines. He considered nature as a self-poised, self-sustaining mechanism, stupendous in its interests, and perfect in its design for the accomplishment of those ultimate ends intended in its organic construction. He had indubitable confidence in Nature, and believed that the existence of all things was secured in a flux and reflux of form from all eternity, and were fashioned by laws permanently adherent in matter, or indissolubly associated therewith.

Thus it was his penchant to regard nature as well worthy of sincere and conscientious thought, and its invisible Author as a pervading element of life, existing in all objects to the desirable end of those diversified relations which are everywhere manifest to the observant senses. Those idealistic considerations which are so characteristic of minds particularly imbued with spiritual comprehension, were either less prominently marked as a peculiarity of his mental organization; or else as a consequence of the multiplied demands made upon his time, as an exponent of moral principles, he hedged in those thoughts which are wont to wander through eternity, and, repudiating all speculative opinions, confined himself more strictly to the establishment of those axiomatic rules, which are the foundation of his ever-practical philosophy.

His chief labor was given to an effort to call the minds of men to an improved condition of social and political life. "I teach you," said Confucius, "only those things which with diligence you might learn yourselves; the recognition of the three fundamental laws of relation between subject and sovereign, father and child, husband and wife; and the five capital virtues—universal charity, impartial justice, conformity to ceremonies and established usages, rectitude of heart and mind, and pure sincerity."

The Confucian system of moral edicts required a strict observance of appointed obligations, and a cultivation of kindly sympathies and sentiments.

The great virtues of charity, justice, and sincerity, were regarded as the only needful religion, securing to the individual, peace, contentment, and happiness, upon earth, and safety from harmful molestation in the life of the future.

Instead of entertaining objections to spiritual faith and discipline, as modernly understood, and as has been asserted by one of his biographers, if not more, the probabilities are that in the absence of all knowledge of Christianity, which in truth had no existence until five hundred years subsequent to the time of Confucius, he taught the most perfect system of philosophy which his understanding enabled him to present, as a comprehensive observer of men and nature, unprovided with modern experience or scientific aids. And while his moral teachings may not, as they do not in the opinion of many, reach the wants and demands of our present spiritual condition, we are quite certain that, as a golden opportunity, the axiomatic school of Confucian precepts furnishes an incentive to the promotion of every desirable good in human character, and leaves but little room for the qualification of those privileges which appertain to the pursuit of a just and noble life.

"Just as I am compelled to accept the manifestations and phenomena of the universe as substantial facts, although I am incompetent to fathom the mystery of their origin; so am I obliged to observe and receive the phenomena of mind in the same light of consideration. We find good and evil, wisdom and ignorance, not only in contrast as between man and man, but as well in our individual characters; the same man is both good and bad, wise and unwise. It is impossible to avoid these distinctions. The principle of righteousness is infiltrated in all nature, and we are forced to recognize it as a paramount and redemptory power. The all-abounding laws of creation, concerning which we know but little more than that they are realities, are governed by its influence, and yield to its control. It is unsafe to entertain mean or deceitful thoughts; for when we offend our own honor, or deride our own consciences, we immolate our better conceptions of goodness, justice, and truth."

Confucius inculcated simple, yet comprehensive rules of life, making them alike applicable to private, as to public requirements. "Let all men," said he, "fashion their lives to accord with the sacred maxims, and make them applicable to the domestic circles wherein they are the responsible advisers; and let them render to the imperial sovereign, who acts as the father of his people, that filial recognition and obedience which is privately demanded by them of their children. We should love, abide by, and honor, the emperor, as it is his custom to love, respect, and venerate, his ancestors; for, by so doing, we are assured of internal peace, social order, and national tranquillity."

Confucius advocated and favored a system of general education; and as a result of plans and measures instituted under his counsel, self-supporting schools were organized throughout the limits of the empire, wherein the moral maxims of the philosopher were taught, and are still imparted as needful to the success of good government and human happiness.

Confucianism appeals to "practical men." It indorses and esteems those virtues which are becoming in the habits and manners of all citizens. It lauds industry, sobriety, gentlemanly decorum, and thoughtfulness. It recognizes toleration of religious opinions, and counsels men to engage in religious service as established from time immemorial, and as a source of piety and respect to the Divine Being. It teaches the existence of genii, or spirits, and recommends sacrificial regard to their interest; as to worship them is demanded, as part of a needful solemnization, bearing on our existence as inheritors of eternal life.

Soon after the death of Confucius, his philosophy was adopted as the State religion, and his maxims were gradually incorporated into the laws of his native land. The entire literary class in China soon accepted his system, and interested themselves in the propagation of the principles which he taught. He did not trust altogether to the memory of his followers for the preservation of his doctrines, but became the author of several books, which were greatly admired by his countrymen for the fine moral sentiments which they contained, and which their author, from motives of modesty, was disinclined to receive any credit for. He very ingeniously avoided accepting the merit of the authorship of the precepts which he taught, by saying that they were of ancient origin, and that he had done nothing more than to collect them from the wise translators, Yao and Chun, who lived fifteen hundred years before his time.

The number of classical or canonical books which he composed, is five; and they are held in the highest esteem, as containing a wise compilation of ancient laws, manners, customs, and practices, and are looked upon as the most perfect rule of government. The first is called the Tih-king, and is a treatise on ethics. The second is the Shu-king, and consists of a history of the deliberations, or advisory councils, which occurred between Ya-ou, Shun, and other personages, who were the ancient kings of the empire, and whose maxims and actions were regarded with sincere veneration. The third canonical book, termed the Shi-king, consists of a compilation of three hundred and eleven sacred songs or poems, which are committed to memory by the Chinese, and repeated on sundry occasions. The Le-king, or Book of Rites, is the foundation of Chinese manners, prescribing all the ceremonies to be observed in the various relationships of life, reflecting upon the cause of the security and stability of Chinese habits, and the permanency of their government. The Chun-tseen is a historical work confined to a narration of events which occurred during his own time, and those immediately preceding him.

Among other books written or compiled by himself and his disciples, may be mentioned the Ta-heo, or Great Study, a political work; the Shung-yung, or "The Invariable in the Mean," a book devoted to teaching what is considered as the "due medium," or "golden mean" in human actions and conduct; the Tun-yu, or "Philosophical Dialogues," containing the recorded conversations of Confucius; and the Hi-tse, composed by Ming-tsi, who died 317 years before Christ, and who was a wise advocate of Confucianism. The object of this work was to inculcate the principles of philanthropic government.

To the works already mentioned we may also add, the Hiao-king, or book containing admonitions in regard to filial reverence, and the replies of Confucius, made in answer to the questions of his disciple Tseng, on the subject of those duties which appertain to a just regard by the young for the counsels of parents; and the Sias-hio, a work devoted to the interests of youthful education in morals.

The Confucian school of philosophy was originally planted in the minds of the aristocratic and educated classes of the Chinese Empire; and its author, unlike all other reformers, labored to imbed his sentiments in the super-stratums of society. And while his success in this particular is as noteworthy as it is wondrous, we cannot say of him as of others, that he rose from poverty and obscurity, making his reputation wholly on the merit of the possession of marvelous talents. For although his teachings may be received as a well-chosen guide for all men, and his system of philosophy as of the most unconstrained and practical kind, the fact of his origin, as being in the line of the nobility of his country, and holding eminent wealth at his command, while it might not detract from the value of the maxims which he delivered to his people, must necessarily dispossess him of that high privilege of renown which would have attached to his name had his efforts rested on the basis of menial domestic relations, purity, and extraordinary mental ability.

Confucius cannot be said to have taught the lesson of spirituality in human life, although it is evident that he recognized the existence of both good and mischievous spirit-beings, as did his ancestors; but he refused to countenance their delivery to mankind as familiar messengers, and only referred to them in the most reserved manner. The questions which most interested him, and to which he gave the most of his attention, were, "*How shall I do my duty to my neigh-*
3

bor," and "*How can I best discharge the duty of a virtuous citizen.*" The subject of the future life was ever hidden in the solemn silence of his own reflections, and, as he thought, was only to be made practical in the great awarding kingdom of Shang-te.

His motives were pure, and his habits were just. He loved to contemplate the principle of goodness as associated with, and reserved to, the practical use of all men. If he possessed any fault which we may discover, or if there is any marked defect in his system of philosophy, it is to be placed to the account of a forgetfulness, or want of knowledge, that all nature is plunged into opposite extremes as a means of self-correction, or cause of justice.

In his reasoning, he was the "plain man," who never hoodwinked his opinions, but against his worldly interests, engaged in fearless trials against a contending opposition to the interests of his *Ma-da-un* * philosophy.

Confucius was beloved and bemoaned by his countrymen, and probably he has left a more lasting impression upon the minds of a greater number of his race, if not of the human family, as a man or representative teacher of worthy morality, than any person who ever lived, or whose name has been handed down to us from the periods of the past. His name is blazoned in the public marts, on the banners of the self-supporting schools, founded and perpetuated on his recommendation, on the altars where the nobility and common people meet to worship, "in the love of justice," and on the monuments raised to his memory in all portions of the empire.

* Amply genial.

A good example for all men, is justly entitled
to the patronage of all men. In his privilege of
life, he was upright, and serenely blessed. No
person has ever presented a nobler record to the
world, or any more justly entitled to universal
confidence. In his daily trials in life, he soberly
met all human abuse with patience, forbearance,
and fortitude. When in his final sorrows and
sufferings, he had attained the summit of the
high mountain of life, and could look down upon
the jargon and contention existing among men,
his highest ambition was still engrossed in a love
of well-doing, and in thinking that he might still
be of service to his people ; but nearing the ter-
mination of his outward career, and feeling his
pulse growing weaker as his end drew nearer, he
rose upon his pillow in the final dream of mind,
and said, " Who shall follow to support my
cause ?" When closing his eyes in unconsciousness
of all outward things, and ceasing to breathe, he
was attended by the "immortals," who conveyed
him onward to the next scene of his labors, in
the spirit-nation of Mongolians, in the *Jung-gee*
of the immortal world.

CONFUCIAN

MORAL PRECEPTS.

1.

THE best method of obtaining intelligence consists in an orderly cultivation of reason and memory, and the acquisition of a knowledge of *things* rather than of *words*, by unceasing industry and perseverance.

2.

When once the mind is thus fixed upon meditation, and yields to a desire for learning, it should reflect concerning those things which pertain to the self-hood of man, or to self-investigation. We should endeavor to obtain some definite idea of *ourselves*, and should observe with earnestness whatever is presented for our consideration; we should examine everything with care, and weigh all things in the balance of reason, then in conformity to a wise decision of mind, we may arrive at the "golden mean" in all our acts in life.

3.

For the improvement of the family circle the parents should take essential care to properly qualify themselves in their habits and manners, and so harmonize their words and actions, as to neither offend good sense, or worthy complaisance. Neither should they in any way allow themselves to become inedifying in the presence of their children or domestics. In order to attain to this exemplary condition of perfection, we must strive to purify our thoughts, subduing our passions and unholy inclinations ; and endeavor to fashion our conduct in the avoidance of contention, vice, misery, mischief, and crime.

4.

To entertain feelings of distrust, love, or aversity; to will, desire, or admire ; we must necessarily abide by the knowledge which we profess; and our impulses, whatever they may be, are sure to be characterized by the *quality* and *amount* of intelligence which we possess.

5.

It is not to be expected that those who know not how to govern themselves, or subdue their own passions, can rightly direct, reform, or govern, others. And it is only those who most struggle for individual improvement that are likely to succeed in accomplishing so desirable a purpose, or who may be depended upon by others in the attainment of that "better condition," which in our moments of sober reflection we all yearn to enjoy.

6.

When we observe a worthy action in another, we should not hesitate to make it our example, or abide by it in practice.

7.

When an opportunity presents itself for well-doing, be earnest in taking immediate advantage of it.

8.

Stay not thy endeavor to suppress or extirpate vice. Always regard your own conduct with discernment and discretion, and keep a vigilant watchfulness over all personal motives, actions, and habits.

9.

Whatsoever is beneficial or honorable, is necessarily advisable; and, as virtue includes both of these qualities, we are obligated in its admiration.

10.

To enjoy and practice virtue in all our actions in life, is to ornament and embellish our manhood and womanhood with the most desirable qualifications.

11.

To the mind, virtue communicates inexpressible beauty and perfection; to the body, it guarantees health, a desirable form, and attractive features. Virtue tranquilizes the heart, and makes ample peace within. It produces a silent, secret joy, calmness and serenity of mind, with an agreeable and kindly appearance which wins the affection of acquaintances, and secures the esteem of the world.

12.

The principal occupation of the mind should be confined to self-investigation and correction. We should endeavor to calm our passions, and hold them under the control of reason. If we suffer ourselves to become angry for some trifling cause, or manifest impetuosity of disposition, we may readily conclude that our condition is defective, and that our standard of rectitude is still imperfect.

13.

If we look upon a person as unworthy of our respect, owing to the manifestation of his defects, and neglect to render justice to his better qualities; if we abandon ourselves to immoderate joy, or submit to be overcome with excessive fear or sorrow; it is justly to be concluded that we have not yet attained to that state of personal rectitude, or disposed harmony of mind, which is so much to be desired, and which is the true foundation of all human happiness.

14.

Let us observe moderation in all things, and hold our passions in abeyance of reasonable reflection.

15.

Let us not blindly yield ourselves to impatience, hastiness, or impetuosity; but reserve our habits and manners to that even-minded way, which is both harmless and acceptable to others, and agreeable to ourselves.

16.

Parents should love each other, and should be governed in their amity by worthy decisions of mind, making their lives conform to evenness and regularity of design.

17.

A son may justly love a father; but, when the father is guilty of the perpetration of any great wrong, or is actuated by unrighteous motives in the pursuit of life, the son should not doubt the propriety of properly remonstrating with his parent, or of acquainting him of his knowledge of the fact, and of advising and counseling him to accept the more commendable way. On the other hand, if a son is inclined to vicious habits, it is the duty of the father to advise and direct him in all matters wherein he is likely to be improved or benefited.

18.

A wise man will always consider his own defects, and diligently labor to remove them.

19.

It is well to conform to the manner and temper of others, only so far as the needful purposes of life are concerned, in our daily dealings and social relations with men. Beyond this we should reserve to ourselves that individual identity of character which is wisely appointed to be our own.

20.

We should never allow ourselves to become corrupted by frivolous conversation, or the example of careless and corrupt persons.

21.

We should never obey the commands of others, or imitate them, without mature reflection.

22.

In our needful association and intercourse with those numerous persons who so unwisely deviate from a worthy standard of moral rectitude, it is better that we turn neither to the right nor left, but follow that "even way" which parries all molestation, and wins all human sympathy.

23.

If a worthy person is chosen to fill some high office in the gift of a people, in a country where virtue is little regarded, and he still continues to cling to his love of morality, or should he preserve all those good habits which characterized his life as a private citizen, refusing to submit to the influence of pride and vanity, then he may be regarded as a man justly entitled to individual respect and national honor.

24.

There are some persons so egotistical in their inclinations as to affect the possession of extraordinary virtue. They pride themselves on the assumption of marvelous goodness, and assume great complaisance in all their actions. "I shall never be enamored with these glittering appearances," says Confucius, "where vanity and self-love have a more marked manifestation than even virtue itself. I would only know and make practical that which it is necessary to know and make practical, as appointed in the demands of everyday life."

25.

There are four general rules, in accordance with the requirements of which a good man should adjust his life:

26.

First, he should regard his father in the same light of "wise intention," in the reception and impartation of kindly advice and counsel, as he would his son.

27.

Second, when serving the interests of the State, he should manifest the same fidelity which he requires of those who serve under him.

28.

Third, It is his duty to love and respect his elder brother, in the same manner as he would expect his younger brother to do toward himself.

29.

Fourth, He should at all times love and respect his friends and acquaintances, as he would have them love and respect him.

30.

The good, wise, and thoughtful man, always acquits himself of these duties with earnestness and fidelity, however ordinary or unseemly they may appear. If he becomes conscious of wrong-doing, or perceives that he has wandered from the "better way," he rests not easy in his own mind, until he has discerned the cause of his mistake, and made his fault the subject of correction. If he discovers that he has neglected an important duty, he will spare no effort or labor which would cancel his neglect, or accomplish the original purpose, which through carelessness or inadvertancy was omitted. He is moderate and reserved in his conversation, and circumspect in his manners. If he feels too great an inclination to social converse, or realizes that he is more affluent of words and ideas than those with whom he speaks, he wisely restrains himself to the limit of needful remark. He is so rigorous a censor of himself, that he at all times endeavors to make his words and his actions correspond. To attain to this condition of individual perfection requires devotional attention to personal habits and virtue.

31.

That love which is requisite for all men to possess, is compounded in our natures, and prompts us alike to filial, parental, and universal, respect for humankind. Our first duty is to love our parents. This filial obedience nurtures our regard for, and prompts us to the practical acceptance of, that universal esteem which has for its object the entire human family. From universal love comes distributive justice, which prompts us to regard all men in the light of "wise understanding," *and to render unto all what is justly their due.*

32.

The difference which exists between the love which we experience toward our parents, and that which we feel toward others; the difference between our regard for the good, the learned, and the wise, and those who are ignorant, impetuous, and degraded in life; should be considered in the light of justice, and characterized by a worthy moderation in our likes and dislikes.

33.

We shall be unable to conform to the necessary rules of life, if we neglect the three pre-eminent virtues: prudence in reflection, which enables us to distinguish between good and bad; universal love, which has regard for the natural rights and interests of all men; and that firm resolution of mind which prompts us to persevere in our adherence to virtue and objections to vice.

34.

Some persons imagine that they are not capable of acquiring virtue, neither of making morality practicable to themselves, whereas it is quite certain that these qualities are attainable by all. And no person who earnestly seeks them, need be deprived of the blessings which they confer. Indeed, it is the impotence and inadvertancy of men which causes them to neglect these interests, or the acquisition of manly habits.

35.

However stupid the individual, or however much wanting in experience, if there exists a desire to learn, and perseverance in study is not attended with weariness or reluctance, the probability is that the person is not far from a worthy prudence in reflection, or success in the exercise of a wise judgment.

36.

If a man, although imbued with strong feelings of self-love, still earnestly endeavors to perform good actions, and acquits himself in justice before men, it may be inferred that he has in a measure already secured the development of that principle of "universal love" within himself, which will induce him to follow the precepts of wisdom in well-doing.

37.

If a man feels the sting of shame when he listens to impure and uncivil conversation, or feels impelled to withdraw from the presence of persons of rude and unpolished manners, it may be safely concluded that he is not far from that condition or resolution of mind which unreservedly indorses goodness, and as strongly objects to vice.

38.

When a person has deviated from the path of integrity or uprightness, it should be his constant effort to restore to himself that confidence which he has lost in the principles of goodness and honor ; by so doing, and by making just atonement through suffering and industry, he will invariably release himself from further inclination in the pursuit of wrong-doing, and rise to a desirable condition in the practice of virtue.

39.

It is most essential that we examine all things with a view to an exact analysis of their properties, qualities, appearances, and effects, for the reason that among those things which are claimed to be known, there are many concerning which the question ever arises as to whether they are perfectly known or not. Hence it becomes necessary to examine them, and to weigh them carefully in the light of every attendant circumstance, as well as to consult the opinion of wise and experienced men thereon.

40.

Notwithstanding it may appear that we clearly understand certain things, including our own natures, still it is evident from the many mistakes which we make, and our numerous transgressions in life, that as individuals we are sadly imperfect, and need to keep a constant vigilance over our own acts. We should meditate not only concerning our own condition, but as well in relation to all surrounding objects and circumstances, being ever watchful and attentive in spirit to the utmost extent whereof we are capable.

41.

We should endeavor to apprehend things aright, reflecting with clearness and precision upon all occasions, to the end that we may avoid all serious mistakes in our decisions of mind, concerning good and bad, the true and the false.

42.

When once we have arrived at a just conclusion, it is our duty to make our acts conform thereunto, and earnestly, as well as unceasingly, endeavor to execute, to the fullest extent of our ability, the good resolution thus decided upon.

43.

If we undertake to perform a duty for another, we should engage in it with the same determination and fidelity of purpose as if we were laboring in our own service.

44.

When visiting with friends, or when in company with worthy associates, regard them with marked sincerity, and be not too reserved in your manifestation of kindness and esteem.

45.

When a man is poor in purse, yet undiminished in honor, or when a man is rich, yet humble, notwithstanding he may be praise-worthy for the rectitude which he manifests, still we cannot say that he has attained the highest degree of virtue, until he becomes absolved from all feelings of impetuosity, cherishing neither hate, fear, malice, nor revenge.

46.

He that is poor should be contented even in the midst of his poverty. He that is rich should be ever charitable, and mindful of well-doing. The penurious and abject spirit does good only to certain persons, gratifies certain exclusive friendships. Such dispense their means only with a view to reaping a reward in material gain; their objects are essentially selfish. Whereas the good man is actuated by generous motives, and qualifies his dealings with men by the light of that wisdom and universal love which holds for its object the interests of all mankind.

47.

We should be ever courteous and kind, even to those who offend us, and especially when they exhibit signs of sincere repentance. We should regard them as if they were innocent of any offense; and, forgetting their imperfections, endeavor, by rendering them aid and encouragement, to prompt them to the pursuit of virtue.

48.

Bemoan not the departed with excessive grief. Not to restrain thy sorrow, is to abandon all reflection, and become lost to a worthy decision of mind.

49.

The wise man never allows himself to be wholly overcome with despair. He rather considers it a weakness than otherwise to yield to immoderate despondency.

50.

The good man never injures himself or others, neither does he lack courage in any emergency. He contemns injuries, gives no credence to reproachful insinuations, and ever refuses to listen to ill reports.

51.

Punishment of crime should neither be too severe nor too common; if magistrates were good men, and if none other were promoted to the dignity of such offices, the common people would reserve themselves to virtuous habits with greater tenacity, because the government of the good and wise is what all men naturally desire; and when we secure the rule of just and competent persons, officers whom all can respect and esteem, we are more willing to abide by approved principles, and in our love of life conform to public approbation.

52.

Hypocrites, or those who profess one thing and practice another, may be compared to professional villains, who, in order to hide their intentions, render themselves wise, and manifest great suavity of manner and disposition during the day, that they may the more effectually conceal the infamy of those crimes which they perpetrate during the night.

53.

Persons who yield to an abuse of their appetites, and constantly indulge in luxurious habits,

4

are unworthy of a rank among men, and are justly
entitled to be called "slaves of the passions," and
" men of brutish inclinations."

54.

Ever make the example of the wise thy hope.
Never allow thyself to become discouraged.
Though thy task become laborious and difficult,
still continue to persevere. If you fail to accomplish the desirable object sought for, remember
that you have the recompense of a consciousness
of having made a commendable effort.

55.

That virtue which is attended with no serious-
ness, is little respected among men.

56.

It is our duty to constantly bear in mind the
important fact that we are frail, and are easily
led from the path of duty.   Hence, should it be
our misfortune to overstep the bounds of propriety, or wander from the righteous way, we should
not be too much disheartened, but endeavor to
rise again above the mischief into which we have
fallen, and secure ourselves from further offending against our individual peace and happiness.

57.

Make all thy promises in justice, and with a
due regard to their fulfillment ; for when we have
committed ourselves to any agreement, it is as unsafe as it is ungenerous, to neglect our duty, or
retract our word.

58.

In conferring homage upon any person, be not overgenerous in its bestowal.

59.

There is stupidity and negligence in too little suavity, and a want of generosity in not properly regarding those persons unto whom we are indebted for either money or favors. To overdo modesty, condescension, or suavity, is equally as great a fault, and involves our manhood or womanhood in ignorance, hypocrisy, conceit, and pride.

60.

Make eating and drinking a consideration in health and comfort, and not a pleasurable gratification, to become the master of all rational conclusions.

61.

Love, temperance, sobriety, and justice. Let your thoughts become purified, and your actions will inevitably correspond therewith.

62.

The attainment of wisdom is the sure guarantee to all desirable pleasure and happiness; and the wise man may find abundant enjoyment in the midst of difficulties and severities.

63.

Those who are studious simply in the reading of books, devoting their time in a great measure to labor and exercise, while neglecting meditation, engage in an unpaying literary pursuit, which adds but little to individual knowledge, and seldom improves the man; while those who are wholly absorbed in meditation, neglecting all exercise, wander and lose themselves in thought, beyond the bound of all proper restraint. The first seldom arrive at any exact conclusions, their opinions being always confounded by doubts and obscurities; while the latter continually pursue the shadows of mind, live in the regions of fancy, and seldom base their knowledge upon anything solid or substantial. It is well to be industrious, but we should never slight meditation. It is desirable to meditate, but let us not neglect the performance of a needful portion of labor.

64.

When any evil exists, and we can discover no remedy for its cure, the better way is to patiently wait for that correction which time affords. If through remonstrances, counsel, and earnest effort, we could succeed in removing it, silence or personal indifference would prove self-abasing. Yet there is nothing more undesirable than the impartation of that advise by which no one is benefited.

65.

Indigence and the miseries of life are unpleasant to endure, but the querulous and the ignorant only resent them and curse Nature for their existence. The wise and the thoughtful only regard Nature as just, and our punishments at her hands quite as needful as they are inevitable. The virtuous man is seldom dissatisfied. His mind compels his spirit to repose in quiet. He allows nothing to disturb his equanimity. His reward is goodness; the practice of a worthy example, his only recompense.

66.

A wise man is always enabled to make a proper choice, as between right and wrong. He may love or distrust with reason, and ever secure a knowledge of justice without discomposure of mind.

67.

He who makes virtue practical in life, never yields to the committal of any act unbecoming a man, or contrary to the decisions of right reason.

68.

Honor and riches are desirable. Nearly all men seek to possess them. But should we discover that honor is impugned or overdone by the possession of wealth, or that riches lead us from the path of rectitude, we should make it our duty to reserve ourselves from their influence, especially wherein they tend to molest us in the pursuit of well-doing, or hamper our happiness in life.

69.

He who taints his mischievous habits with pride and conceit, and is neither frugal nor careful with his means, is seldom disposed for the study of wisdom. Sociable familiarity with such persons is not to be commended.

70.

Feel not afflicted because thou art not promoted to grandeur and public dignities. It were better to grieve that thou art lacking those virtues which might render thee worthy of being advanced.

71.

The good man devotes his life to the practice of virtue; the bad man neglects its pursuit in his struggle for wealth. The first cherishes a love for goodness, admires wisdom, and contemplates the public welfare. The latter is absorbed with local and selfish cares, and thinks only concerning those matters which pertain to his selfish interests.

72.

The good man no sooner observes a person of wise inclinations than he endeavors to imitate his worthy example.

73.

When a good man observes a person of vicious habits, he wisely reflects concerning himself, with a view to the discovery and removal of any similar defects which he may possess, and which he so much detests in others.

74.

Children are in duty bound to obey and serve, in all reasonableness, the requirements of their parents. Sometimes parents are sadly at fault. It is proper for children to acquaint them therewith, but it should be done with care and prudence. Should the child meet with opposition or anger, he should exercise patience, delaying for a time his purpose, but should, when a good opportunity offers, persist in his effort. Advice given to parents is frequently attended with unjust punishments to the child. Resistance can only be justified in extreme cases. Usually we should suffer without complaining.

75.

The wise man is always moderate in his studies, also in his actions and conversation. He is often silent, but when it is needful for him to be in haste, he makes it his purpose to speak or act with precipitancy and force.

76.

To properly understand the character of a person, we need to have association with them, and reflect upon their peculiarities. "When I was young," says Confucius, "I imagined that all men were honest and sincere; that their practical habits conformed to their utterances. But since I have grown to manhood, I behold things in another light. I am satisfied that I was mistaken. I now listen to what men have to say, and place only that confidence therein, which, with proper reservation of mind, the subject seems to demand. I examine whether men's words conform to their actions, and refuse to content myself with external appearances."

77.

Parental imperfections should not debar children from private or public respect. If in consequence of the committal of crimes or misdemeanor, a father should render himself ineligible to office, or unworthy of human confidence, his conduct should be no cause of disgrace to his children, neither should they be refused that society which their good manners justly entitle them to. If a son is born of poor parents, or is of obscure birth, it should be made no excuse for objections to his success; but, on the contrary, his ample qualification should secure him the same employment which would be conferred upon the rich.

78.

Poverty or imprisonment are preferable to the most eminent offices of government, when they are conferred and managed by agents or rulers who are malicious, knavish or untrustworthy; and he who accepts them is most likely to confound personal blessings with selfish interest, and in the end is certain to regret his action, from disappointment and displeasure.

79.

The path that leadeth to virtue is broad and secure, and it is our duty to relinquish no effort which would enable us to keep in its course. We should not complain of a want of strength, nor allege that difficulties discourage us, but determinately pursue the object of our regard, in the face of all disheartening circumstances.

80.

It is not enough to know virtue; it is necessary to possess it. It is not sufficient to admire it; it is necessary to practice it.

81.

He who engages in persecution against a good man, chooses war against the best interests of community, and derides his own character and happiness.

82.

Children should be in constant watchfulness over their own acts, and endeavor to avoid afflicting, offending, or displeasing, their parents; this thought should be constantly uppermost in their minds.

83.

As the most desirable health is endangered by living in a malarious atmosphere; so is our claim to godliness canceled by association with those who are vicious and degraded.

84.

Sincerity and constancy of mind are a sure guarantee to a reputation for worth and sobriety, and constantly add to our happiness, notwithstanding our severest trials and difficulties in life.

85.

The wise man always takes counsel, sometimes consulting even the least-intelligent persons, when important affairs demand an immediate decision of judgment. When counsel is good, we should accept it, although it should come from an unexpected and seemingly exceptionable source.

86.

Vanity, haughtiness, and pride, should always be avoided. While thou mayest claim that prudence and ability which the ancients possessed, still, if thou art not humble, frank, generous, considerate, and agreeable, thou art likely to be looked upon as selfish and worldly, and contemned as a person of sordid inclinations.

87.

Consider what thou already knowest; it is beneficial to restore memory by a rehearsal of past experience. We are apt to overlook our own defects, and deride others for imperfections which we neglect to observe in ourselves.

88.

Do nothing ungenerous, unkind, or unjust, although thou art competent to make thine acts approved. Deception may find security for a time, but never permanent justification.

89.

Engage no lasting friendships with men, when their company would endanger your personal reputation, or their presence become derisive of your sense of propriety.

90.

A considerate man is likely to blush at his own faults, but is never averse to their correction.

91.

All worthy aspiration is unaccompanied by envy, covetousness, or greed.

92.

Wouldst thou learn to die contentedly, learn thou first to live wisely.

93.

Give of thy superabundance to the poor.

94.

Make frank acknowledgment of all benefits received, by the return of other benefits equally to be desired.

95.

When we make a conquest over our personal defects, we secure the most worthy victory in life.

96.

In doing something to make others happy, we are conceding life to be a joy worthy of our trust and confidence.

97.

Let us freely confess our faults and mistakes, and thus reserve ourselves to honor and sincerity.

98.

Let us watch diligently and not lose our better opportunities. If we fall behind in the pursuit of virtue, we may be longer in securing it, and our sufferings in life may be thereby augmented.

99.

To justly regard those who wrong or injure you, without entertaining feelings of anger, hate, or revenge, is indisputable evidence of the possession of worthy wisdom, and of a manifestation of the spirit of true religion.

100.

Do unto another what you would he should do unto you; and do not unto another what you would not should be done unto you. Thou needest only this law alone; it is the foundation and principle of all the rest.

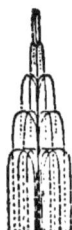

THE

MASTEREON:

Being a treatise on the *Du-al-vi-lon* of Nature, as presented in the external and spiritual relations of matter and mind.

BY

MARCENUS R. K. WRIGHT.

The above work is designed to present a new theory concerning the origin of all natural manifestations, and a comprehensive explanation of spirit phenomena. It is written from an *Interior* stand-point of view, and will be supported by the best aids which science and philosophy can confer. It will be issued in a series of 12mo volumes, at the uniform price of $1.50 each. In the "Mastereon," nature will be regarded as our "only hope," and we shall make it our duty to criticize those subjects and opinions which come within the sphere of our needful consideration, with freedom and fearlessness, yet with candor and sincerity.

It is designed to investigate the subject of the natural manifestations of the outward world, and their relations to an interior, active cause, and to demonstrate the existence of an *In-te-un* sphere of life, fashioned in the elements of the aerial hights above us, in a manner to conform to principles substantially logical and scientific. It will also contain articles upon various subjects, including the Human Mind, Psychology, Clairvoyance, The Future Life, The Principle of Will, Spirit Communications, and a number of biographical sketches, wherein will be given the details of a most singular personal experience.

Subscriptions to the Mastereon are solicited. All names received will be registered. A deduction of 25 cents will be made from the retail price upon each volume sent to subscribers, who will receive a circular as soon as the first volume is published.

Address M. R. K. WRIGHT,
Middleville, Barry Co., Mich.